10 KEYS
to
MAXIMIZING
Your
HEAVENLY
FICO SCORES
WORKBOOK

TRANSFORMING YOUR LIFE
THROUGH BIBLICAL PRINCIPLES

DONNIE RAY FEATHERSTONE, SR.

Largo, MD

Copyright © 2024 Donnie Ray Featherstone, Sr.

All rights reserved under the international copyright law. No part of this book may be reproduced or transmitted in any form or by any means, electronic or mechanical, including photocopying, recording, or by any information storage and retrieval system, without the express, written permission of the publisher or the author. The exception is reviewers, who may quote brief passages in a review.

Christian Living Books, Inc.
ChristianLivingBooks.com
We bring your dreams to fruition.

ISBN 9781562296469

All Scripture quotations are taken from The New King James Version / Thomas Nelson Publishers, Nashville: Thomas Nelson Publishers, Copyright © 1982. Used by permission. All rights reserved worldwide.

Table of Contents

Introduction *1*

Chapter 1: Faith That Moves God 2

Chapter 2: Distinct Identity 5

Chapter 3: Next-Level Commitment 8

Chapter 4: Obedience Is the Key 11

Chapter 5: Sanctification Is a Process 14

Chapter 6: The Power of Change 17

Chapter 7: Obligation Without Hesitation 20

Chapter 8: Righteousness Is a Choice 23

Chapter 9: You Can Excel 26

Chapter 10: The Responsibility of Stewardship 29

Conclusion *32*

Introduction

Maximizing your heavenly FICO SCORES is a journey of transformation, growth, and deepening intimacy with God. This workbook is designed to be a tool for personal growth and a catalyst for change. It is not just about acquiring knowledge or completing exercises but rather about experiencing God's life-changing presence and allowing Him to shape you into the person He created you to be.

1. **Get a journal**: We've provided space for key fields but be sure to keep your dedicated journal nearby. It's where you can freely capture your thoughts, revelations, and growth desires without limits. This way, you have all the room you need to truly engage in your journey.

2. **Set aside dedicated time**: Choose a time each day or week to work through the chapters and exercises. Consistency is key to spiritual growth.

3. **Pray for guidance**: Before you begin each chapter, pray for God's wisdom, revelation, and guidance as you work through the material.

4. **Reflect and respond**: Take time to thoughtfully answer the questions and complete the exercises. Be honest with yourself and with God about your struggles, desires, and areas for growth.

5. **Memorize scripture**: Each chapter includes a "Word Wealth Builder" with a key scripture to memorize. Hide these verses in your heart and meditate on them throughout your day.

6. **Apply the principles**: Look for opportunities to put the principles and strategies you learn into practice in your daily life. Real transformation happens when you move from knowledge to application.

7. **Share your journey**: Consider finding a prayer partner, accountability group, or mentor with whom you can share your journey. Encourage and support one another as you grow in your faith.

Remember, this workbook is a tool, but the real transformation comes from your relationship with God and your willingness to surrender to His will. Approach each chapter with an open heart, expecting God to speak to you and work in your life. Trust in His faithfulness and goodness, knowing that He is committed to your growth and transformation. May this workbook be a blessing to you as you seek to maximize your heavenly FICO SCORES and experience the abundant life God has for you.

Chapter 1: Faith That Moves God

Faith is the foundation of our relationship with God. It is the unwavering belief in His promises, even when our circumstances seem to contradict them. In this chapter, we will explore the power of faith and how it can move the heart of God, drawing us closer to Him and unlocking the abundant blessings He has in store for us.

Credit Repair

1. What areas of your life require a "faith repair"? In what situations do you struggle to trust God fully?

_____
_____
_____

2. How have your past experiences or disappointments affected your ability to have faith in God's promises?

_____
_____
_____

3. What practical steps can you take to strengthen your faith and trust in God, even amid challenging circumstances?

_____
_____
_____

Savings Deposit

1. Recall when you stepped out in faith and saw God come through for you. How did that experience impact your faith?

_____
_____
_____

2. What are some of the promises of God that you can hold onto and "deposit" into your heart when your faith is wavering?

_____
_____
_____

3. How can you intentionally "invest" in your faith by spending time in God's Word, prayer, and fellowship with other believers?

_____

_____

_____

_____

Investment Portfolio

1. What are some areas in your life where you need to "invest" more faith (e.g., relationships, career, ministry, etc.)?

_____

_____

_____

2. How can you diversify your "faith portfolio" by trusting God in the big and small areas of your life?

_____

_____

_____

_____

3. What are the potential "returns" or blessings that come from investing faith in God and His plans for your life?

_____

_____

_____

_____

Word Wealth Builder

> *"Now faith is the substance of things hoped for, the evidence of things not seen." (Hebrews 11:1 NKJV)*

Faith is the confident assurance that what we hope for will happen; it gives us certainty about things we cannot see. This verse reminds us that true faith is anchored in God's trustworthiness and promises, even when our physical senses cannot perceive the outcome.

Growth Fund

1. How has your faith grown or matured over the past year? What experiences or lessons have contributed to that growth?

   _____
   _____
   _____
   _____

2. In what areas do you desire to see further growth in your faith? What steps can you take to facilitate that growth?

   _____
   _____
   _____
   _____

3. How can you use your faith journey to encourage and inspire growth in the lives of others?

   _____
   _____
   _____
   _____

Optimization Strategy

Keep a faith journal this week. Each day, write down one situation where you choose to trust God, even in the face of uncertainty or challenges. At the end of the week, reflect on how exercising your faith has impacted your perspective, peace, and relationship with God.

Prayer Maximizer

Father, I come before You today with a heart full of gratitude and expectation. I thank You for being a faithful God whose promises never fail. Help me to fix my eyes on You, the author and perfecter of my faith. When doubts and fears assail me, remind me of Your unfailing love and unshakable trustworthiness. Give me the courage to step out in obedience, even when the path ahead is uncertain. Stretch my faith, Lord, and use me to accomplish Your purposes. May my life be a testament to the power of faith, and may I experience the fullness of Your blessings as I trust in You. In Jesus' name, Amen.

Chapter 2: Distinct Identity

Our identity is one of the most crucial aspects of our spiritual journey. It shapes our thoughts, actions, and the way we perceive ourselves and others. In a world that often tries to define us by our failures, circumstances, or the opinions of others, it is essential to understand that our true identity is found in Christ.

Credit Repair

1. How have past hurts, failures, or negative experiences shaped your identity and how you see yourself?

_____

_____

_____

2. In what ways have you allowed the opinions of others or societal expectations to define your identity?

_____

_____

_____

3. What truths from God's Word can you use to "repair" any faulty beliefs about your identity and replace them with the truth of who you are in Christ?

_____

_____

_____

Savings Deposit

1. List the positive attributes, gifts, and strengths that God has placed within you. How can you "deposit" these into your life and the lives of others?

_____

_____

_____

2. What are some of the biblical promises and affirmations about your identity in Christ that you can meditate on and "save" in your heart?

_____

_____

_____

3. How can you cultivate a habit of speaking life and truth over yourself, "saving" up a reservoir of positive self-talk rooted in your identity in God?

___

___

___

Investment Portfolio

1. What practical ways can you "invest" in your God-given identity (e.g., developing your talents, serving others, pursuing personal growth)?

___

___

___

___

2. How can you "diversify" your understanding of your identity by exploring the various aspects of who you are in Christ (e.g., beloved child, masterpiece, overcomer)?

___

___

___

___

3. What are the eternal "returns" from investing in your true identity and living out your God-given purpose?

___

___

___

___

Word Wealth Builder

> *"Therefore, if anyone is in Christ, he is a new creation; old things have passed away; behold, all things have become new." (2 Corinthians 5:17 NKJV)*

This powerful verse reminds us that when we are in Christ, we are not defined by our past mistakes or the labels placed upon us by the world. Instead, we are made new, with a distinct identity as children of God, empowered to live a life of purpose and transformation.

Growth Fund

1. Reflect on your spiritual journey. How has your understanding of your identity in Christ grown and evolved?

   _____
   _____
   _____
   _____

2. In what areas do you desire further growth in understanding and acceptance of your true identity?

   _____
   _____
   _____
   _____

3. How can you use your journey of discovering your identity to help others grow in their understanding of who they are in Christ?

   _____
   _____
   _____
   _____

Optimization Strategy

Create an "Identity Declaration" card. Write down 3-5 fundamental truths about your identity in Christ (e.g., "I am accepted," "I am forgiven," "I am loved unconditionally"). Place this card in a prominent place where you will see it daily, such as on your bathroom mirror or wallet. Read these declarations aloud each day, affirming your true identity in God.

Prayer Maximizer

Father, I come before You today, recognizing that my true identity is in You alone. I thank You for creating me in Your image, with purpose and destiny. Forgive me for the times I have allowed the world to shape my identity rather than Your truth. Help me to see myself through Your eyes—as a beloved child, chosen and set apart for Your glory. Give me the courage to embrace my distinct identity and to live out the unique calling You have placed on my life. May I find my confidence, security, and worth in You alone, knowing that nothing can separate me from Your unfailing love. Use me, Lord, to reflect Your light and love to a world in need as I walk in the fullness of who I am in You. In Jesus' name, Amen.

Chapter 3: Next-Level Commitment

Commitment is a crucial aspect of our spiritual growth and a key factor in raising our heavenly FICO SCORES. It is the unwavering dedication to God and His purposes, even in the face of challenges and obstacles. In this chapter, we will explore what it means to take our commitment to the next level and how this can deepen our relationship with God and unlock His blessings in our lives.

Credit Repair

1. In what areas of your life do you struggle with commitment? How has this affected your spiritual growth?

___

2. What are some of the barriers or excuses that prevent you from fully committing to God and His plans for your life?

___

3. What practical steps can you take to "repair" any areas of weak commitment and cultivate a wholehearted devotion to Christ?

___

Savings Deposit

1. Reflect on a time when you demonstrated unwavering commitment, even in the face of challenges. What lessons did you learn from that experience?

___

2. What are some of the biblical examples of commitment that inspire you? How can you "deposit" these examples into your own life?

___

3. How can you "invest" in your commitment to God by setting aside regular time for prayer, worship, and service?

___

Investment Portfolio

1. What are some specific areas in your life where you need to "invest" more commitment (e.g., prayer, Bible study, serving others)?

___

2. How can you "diversify" your commitment by being faithful in the big and small responsibilities God has entrusted you?

___

3. What are the long-term "returns" of investing in a life of commitment to God and His purposes?

___

Word Wealth Builder

> *"But seek first the kingdom of God and His righteousness, and all these things shall be added to you." (Matthew 6:33 NKJV)*

This verse reminds us that when we prioritize God and His purposes, He will care for all our needs. By committing to seek His kingdom first, we position ourselves to experience His provision and blessings in every area of our lives.

Growth Fund

1. How has your level of commitment to God grown over the past year? What experiences or lessons have contributed to that growth?

   _____
   _____
   _____
   _____

2. In what areas do you desire to see further growth in your commitment? What steps can you take to facilitate that growth?

   _____
   _____
   _____
   _____

3. How can you use your journey of growing in commitment to encourage and inspire others in their walk with God?

   _____
   _____
   _____
   _____

Optimization Strategy

Create a "Commitment Action Plan." Identify one area where you want to grow in your commitment to God (e.g., spending more time in prayer or serving in your local church). Break this goal into small, manageable steps and create a timeline for implementing these steps over the next month. Share your plan with a trusted friend or accountability partner who can support you in your journey.

Prayer Maximizer

Father, I come before You today with a heart desiring to go deeper in my commitment to You. I acknowledge that You are worthy of my wholehearted devotion and surrender. Forgive me for the times I have allowed other pursuits or priorities to take Your place in my life. Give me the strength and courage to put You first, no matter the cost. Help me to trust in Your unfailing love and faithfulness, knowing that as I commit my ways to You, You will direct my paths. Ignite within me a passion for Your presence and a zeal for Your purposes. May my life be marked by an unwavering commitment to You as I seek to glorify Your name in all I do. In Jesus' name, Amen.

Chapter 4: Obedience Is the Key

Obedience is a fundamental aspect of our relationship with God and a vital key to unlocking His blessings in our lives. It is the act of submitting our will to His and choosing to follow His commands, even when it may be difficult or counter-cultural. In this chapter, we will explore the power of obedience and how it can transform our lives and deepen our connection with our Heavenly Father.

Credit Repair

1. In what areas of your life do you struggle with obedience to God? What are the root causes of this disobedience?

   _____
   _____
   _____

2. How have past experiences or wounds affected your ability to trust and obey God fully?

   _____
   _____
   _____

3. What practical steps can you take to "repair" any areas of disobedience and cultivate a heart responsive to God's leading?

   _____
   _____
   _____

Savings Deposit

1. Recall a time when you chose to obey God, even when challenged. How did that act of obedience impact your faith and relationship with Him?

   _____
   _____

2. What are some of the biblical promises and blessings associated with obedience that you can "deposit" into your heart and mind?

   _____
   _____

3. How can you "invest" in your obedience by memorizing and meditating on scriptures that encourage and empower you to follow God's commands?

___

Investment Portfolio

1. What are some specific areas in your life where you need to "invest" more obedience (e.g., relationships, finances, ministry)?

___

2. How can you "diversify" your obedience by being faithful in both the public and private aspects of your walk with God?

___

3. What are the eternal "returns" of investing in a life of obedience and submission to God's will?

___

Word Wealth Builder

"If you love Me, keep My commandments." (John 14:15 NKJV)

This simple yet profound verse reminds us that our obedience is an expression of our love for God. When we follow His commands, we demonstrate our devotion and trust in Him, deepening our relationship and opening the door for His blessings to flow in our lives.

Growth Fund

1. Reflect on your journey of learning to obey God. How has your understanding and practice of obedience grown over time?

   _____
   _____
   _____
   _____

2. In what areas do you desire to see further growth in your obedience? What steps can you take to facilitate that growth?

   _____
   _____
   _____
   _____

3. How can you use your experiences and growth in obedience to mentor and encourage others in their walk with God?

   _____
   _____
   _____
   _____

Optimization Strategy

Conduct an "Obedience Audit." Reflect on your life prayerfully and identify areas where you may struggle with obedience to God. Write these down, and then, next to each one, write a corresponding action step you can take to align your life with God's will in that area. Commit to implementing these action steps over the next week, and trust God to empower you as you seek to obey Him.

Prayer Maximizer

Father, I come before You today with a heart longing to obey You. I acknowledge that Your ways are higher than mine and Your thoughts higher than mine. Forgive me for the times I have chosen my path instead of Yours. Give me the wisdom to discern Your will and the courage to follow it, even when it is difficult. Help me to trust in Your goodness and love, knowing that Your commands are for my protection and blessing. Empower me by Your Holy Spirit to walk in obedience, not out of fear or obligation, but out of a deep love and devotion to You. May my life be a living testimony of the joy and freedom of surrendering to Your perfect will. In Jesus' name, Amen.

Chapter 5: Sanctification Is a Process

Sanctification, the process of being set apart for God's purposes and growing in holiness, is a lifelong journey that lies at the heart of our spiritual growth. It is not a one-time event, but a continuous transformation that requires patience, perseverance, and a deep reliance on God's grace. In this chapter, we will explore the significance of sanctification and how it relates to raising our heavenly FICO SCORES.

Credit Repair

1. In what areas of your life do you feel stuck or stagnant in your spiritual growth? What might be hindering your sanctification process?

    _____
    _____
    _____

2. How have past failures or setbacks affected your view of yourself and your potential for growth and transformation?

    _____
    _____
    _____

3. What truths from God's Word can you use to "repair" any faulty beliefs about your identity and potential in Christ?

    _____
    _____
    _____

Savings Deposit

1. Reflect on a time when you experienced significant growth or breakthrough in your sanctification journey. What lessons did you learn from that experience?

    _____
    _____

2. What are some of the biblical promises and truths about God's transformative power that you can "deposit" into your heart and mind?

    _____
    _____

3. How can you "invest" in your sanctification by cultivating spiritual disciplines such as prayer, fasting, and scripture meditation?

___

Investment Portfolio

1. What are some specific areas of your character or behavior where you need to "invest" more effort in your sanctification process?

___

2. How can you "diversify" your approach to sanctification by addressing growth in various aspects of your life (e.g., thoughts, emotions, relationships)?

___

3. What are the long-term "returns" of investing in your sanctification and allowing God to transform you from the inside out?

___

Word Wealth Builder

> *"Being confident of this very thing, that He who has begun a good work in you will complete it until the day of Jesus Christ." (Philippians 1:6 NKJV)*

This encouraging verse reminds us that our sanctification is ultimately God's work in us. As we cooperate with His Spirit and surrender to His transformative power, we can have confidence that He will continue to shape us into the image of Christ until His return.

Growth Fund

1. How has your understanding and experience of sanctification grown over the past year? What challenges or victories have shaped your perspective?

_____
_____
_____
_____

2. In what areas do you desire further growth in your sanctification journey? What practical steps can you take to facilitate that growth?

_____
_____
_____
_____

3. How can you use your own story of transformation to encourage and inspire others in their sanctification process?

_____
_____
_____
_____

Optimization Strategy

Develop a "Sanctification Plan." Identify one area where you desire growth and transformation (e.g., overcoming a particular sin, developing a fruit of the Spirit). Create a plan that includes regular prayer, relevant scripture study, accountability with a trusted friend, and practical action steps. Commit to following this plan for the next month, keeping a journal to track your progress and insights.

Prayer Maximizer

Father, I come before You today, acknowledging that sanctification is a lifelong process that requires Your constant grace and transformative power. I thank You for the work You have begun in me, and I trust You to complete it. Forgive me for the times I have resisted Your refining fire or grown discouraged in the face of challenges. Renew my mind and heart, aligning them with Your truth and purpose. Give me the strength to persevere when the process is painful, knowing that You are shaping me into the likeness of Your Son. Fill me with Your Holy Spirit, enabling me to walk in increasing measures of holiness and obedience. May my life reflect Your beauty and goodness as I grow in intimacy with You and impact the world around me for Your glory. In Jesus' name, Amen.

Chapter 6: The Power of Change

Change is an inevitable and essential part of our spiritual journey. It is the process of transformation that occurs as we surrender our lives to Christ and allow His Spirit to work in us. In this chapter, we will explore the power of change and how embracing it can lead to a deeper relationship with God and a more fulfilling life.

Credit Repair

1. In what areas do you resist change or struggle to let go of old patterns and habits?

___

2. How have past negative experiences or fear of the unknown affected your willingness to embrace change?

___

3. What truths from God's Word can you use to "repair" any faulty beliefs or attitudes about change and its role in your spiritual growth?

___

Savings Deposit

1. Reflect on when you experienced a significant change in your life and how God used that change to bring about growth and blessing.

___

2. What are some biblical promises and truths about God's transformative power and His plans for your life that you can "deposit" into your heart and mind?

___

3. How can you "invest" in your capacity for change by cultivating an open and teachable spirit and seeking godly wisdom and counsel?

___

Investment Portfolio

1. What are some specific areas of your life where you need to "invest" more willingness to change and grow (e.g., attitudes, relationships, habits)?

___

2. How can you "diversify" your approach to change by being open to God's leading in various aspects of your life, both big and small?

___

3. What are the long-term "returns" of investing in a life open to change and growth, both personally and in your impact on others?

___

Word Wealth Builder

"Do not be conformed to this world, but be transformed by the renewing of your mind, that you may prove what is that good and acceptable and perfect will of God." (Romans 12:2 NKJV)

This powerful verse reminds us that change begins with a transformation of our minds. As we allow God's Word and Spirit to renew our thinking and align it with His will, we experience the power of change in every area of our lives.

Growth Fund

1. How has your understanding and experience of change grown over the past year? What lessons have you learned about embracing transformation?

   _____
   _____
   _____
   _____

2. In what areas do you desire further growth in navigating and embracing change? What steps can you take to facilitate that growth?

   _____
   _____
   _____
   _____

3. How can you use your own story of transformation to encourage and inspire others facing the challenges of change in their lives?

   _____
   _____
   _____
   _____

Optimization Strategy

Embark on a "Change Challenge." Identify one area of your life where you sense God calling you to make a significant change (e.g., a habit, a relationship, a mindset). Commit to taking one small step each day for 30 days to move towards that change. Keep a journal to record your progress, struggles, and insights. Celebrate your growth and trust God to continue the transformative work He has begun in you.

Prayer Maximizer

Father, I come before You today, recognizing that change is a necessary and powerful part of my journey with You. I thank You for the transformative work You are doing in my life, molding me into the image of Your Son. Forgive me for the times I have resisted change or clung to old patterns and habits that hindered my growth. Give me the courage to embrace the new things You are doing, even when it feels uncomfortable or uncertain. Help me to trust in Your goodness and faithfulness, knowing that Your plans for me are always for my benefit and Your glory. Renew my mind and heart, aligning them with Your truth and empowering me to walk in the fullness of the change You desire. May my life be a testament to the transformative power of Your love and grace as I continually surrender to Your holy purposes. In Jesus' name, Amen.

Chapter 7: Obligation Without Hesitation

Obligation, the act of fulfilling our responsibilities and commitments, is a vital aspect of our spiritual lives. It is the willingness to serve God and others without hesitation, even when it may be inconvenient or challenging. In this chapter, we will explore the significance of obligation and how it relates to raising our heavenly FICO SCORES.

Credit Repair

1. In what areas of your life do you struggle to fulfill your obligations or follow through on your commitments?

___

2. How have past failures or negative experiences affected your view of obligation and your ability to serve without hesitation?

___

3. What truths from God's Word can you use to "repair" any faulty beliefs or attitudes about obligation and its role in your spiritual growth?

___

Savings Deposit

1. Reflect on a time when you willingly fulfilled an obligation or served others, even when it was challenging. What lessons did you learn from that experience?

___

2. What are some biblical promises and truths about the blessings and rewards of faithful service that you can "deposit" into your heart and mind?

___

3. How can you "invest" in your capacity for obligation by cultivating a heart of humility, compassion, and willingness to serve?

Investment Portfolio

1. What are some specific areas of your life where you need to "invest" more willingness to serve and fulfill your obligations (e.g., family, work, ministry)?

2. How can you "diversify" your approach to obligation by being open to serving in various capacities and settings as God leads?

3. What are the long-term "returns" of investing in a life characterized by faithful service and unwavering commitment to your responsibilities?

Word Wealth Builder

> *"And whatever you do, do it heartily, as to the Lord and not to men, knowing that from the Lord you will receive the reward of the inheritance; for you serve the Lord Christ." (Colossians 3:23-24 NKJV)*

This inspiring passage reminds us that every obligation and act of service, no matter how small or mundane, is an opportunity to serve Christ Himself. As we approach our duties with love and dedication, we store eternal rewards and bring glory to God.

Growth Fund

1. How has your understanding and practice of obligation grown over the past year? What challenges or victories have shaped your perspective?

_____

_____

_____

_____

2. In what areas do you desire further growth in your ability to serve and fulfill your commitments without hesitation? What steps can you take to facilitate that growth?

_____

_____

_____

_____

3. How can you use your learning journey to serve faithfully and encourage and inspire others in their walk with God?

_____

_____

_____

_____

Optimization Strategy

Conduct an "Obligation Inventory." Prayerfully reflect on the various responsibilities and commitments God has entrusted you (e.g., family roles, work duties, ministry involvement). Write each one down and then, next to each, rate your current level of faithfulness and enthusiasm in fulfilling that obligation. Identify areas where you need to grow and commit to taking one practical step this week to serve with greater dedication and joy in those areas.

Prayer Maximizer

Father, I come before You today, recognizing that every obligation and responsibility I have is an opportunity to serve and glorify You. I thank You for the privilege of being Your hands and feet in this world, demonstrating Your love and compassion to those around me. Forgive me for the times I have neglected my duties or served with a grudging heart. Renew my mind and attitude, aligning them with Your heart of joyful service and unwavering commitment. Give me the strength and grace to fulfill my obligations with excellence, even when challenging or inconvenient. Help me see every act of service as an act of worship to You, storing eternal treasures in heaven. May my life be marked by a spirit of faithful obligation, bringing honor to Your name and drawing others to the beauty of Your love. In Jesus' name, Amen.

Chapter 8: Righteousness Is a Choice

Righteousness, or right standing with God, is often viewed as an unattainable standard or a status reserved for the spiritually elite. However, the truth is that righteousness is a choice available to every believer through faith in Jesus Christ. In this chapter, we will explore the concept of righteousness and how it impacts our heavenly FICO SCORES.

Credit Repair

1. In what areas of your life do you struggle to make righteous choices or live up to God's standards?

___

2. How have past failures or a sense of unworthiness affected your view of righteousness and your ability to receive it as a gift?

___

3. What truths from God's Word can you use to "repair" any faulty beliefs or attitudes about righteousness and your standing before God?

___

Savings Deposit

1. Reflect on when you experienced the joy and freedom of living in right standing with God. What lessons did you learn from that experience?

___

2. What are some biblical promises and truths about the benefits of righteousness that you can "deposit" into your heart and mind?

___

3. How can you "invest" in your righteousness by cultivating a deep love for God and a desire to honor Him in every area of your life?

Investment Portfolio

1. What are some specific areas of your life where you need to "invest" more in making righteous choices and living according to God's standards?

2. How can you "diversify" your approach to righteousness by seeking to honor God in various aspects of your life, both public and private?

3. What are the long-term "returns" of investing in a life of righteousness and aligning your choices with God's will?

Word Wealth Builder

> *"For He made Him who knew no sin to be sin for us, that we might become the righteousness of God in Him." (2 Corinthians 5:21 NKJV)*

This powerful verse encapsulates the heart of the gospel message. Through Christ's sacrificial death on the cross, our sins were placed upon Him, and His perfect righteousness was imputed to us. As we put our faith in Him, we are clothed in His righteousness and made acceptable in God's sight.

Growth Fund

1. How has your understanding and experience of righteousness grown over the past year? What challenges or victories have shaped your perspective?

   _____
   _____
   _____
   _____

2. In what areas do you desire further growth in your ability to live righteously and honor God with your choices? What steps can you take to facilitate that growth?

   _____
   _____
   _____
   _____

3. How can you use your learning journey to live righteously to encourage and inspire others in their walk with God?

   _____
   _____
   _____
   _____

Optimization Strategy

Create a "Righteousness Reset" plan. Identify one area of your life where you consistently struggle to make righteous choices. Develop a practical strategy for overcoming temptation and aligning your decisions with God's will. This plan might include memorizing relevant scriptures, seeking accountability with a trusted friend, and establishing healthy boundaries. Commit to implementing this plan for 30 days, keeping a journal to track your progress and insights.

Prayer Maximizer

Father, I come before You today, humbled and grateful for the gift of righteousness that is mine through faith in Your Son, Jesus Christ. I thank You for the incredible exchange that took place on the cross — my sins for His perfect righteousness. Forgive me for the times I have relied on my efforts or merit to achieve right standing with You. Help me to fully embrace the truth that my righteousness is a result of Your grace alone. Give me the wisdom and strength to make righteous choices in every area of my life, honoring You with my thoughts, words, and actions. May my life be a testament to the transformative power of Your righteousness as I walk in increasing measures of holiness and obedience. Use me as an instrument of Your righteousness in this world, shining Your light and drawing others to the beauty of Your saving grace. In Jesus' name, Amen.

Chapter 9: You Can Excel

Excellence is a journey, not a destination. It's not about being flawless or achieving a specific status; instead, it's about consistently striving to be better and making the most of the talents and opportunities God has given us. In this chapter, we will explore the concept of excellence through the lens of spiritual growth and discover how anyone can excel in their walk with God, ultimately leading to an increase in their heavenly FICO SCORES.

Credit Repair

1. In what areas of your life do you struggle with feelings of inadequacy or a belief that you cannot excel?

   _____
   _____
   _____

2. How have past failures or negative experiences affected your view of your potential and ability to achieve excellence?

   _____
   _____
   _____

3. What truths from God's Word can you use to "repair" any faulty beliefs or attitudes about your God-given abilities and potential?

   _____
   _____
   _____

Savings Deposit

1. Reflect on when you experienced the joy and satisfaction of excelling in a particular area or task. What lessons did you learn from that experience?

   _____
   _____
   _____

2. What are some biblical promises and truths about God's desire for us to excel and the resources He provides to help us do so?

   _____
   _____

3. How can you "invest" in your pursuit of excellence by cultivating a growth mindset and a willingness to learn and develop your skills and abilities?

___

Investment Portfolio

1. What areas of your life do you feel God is calling you to pursue excellence and develop your skills and abilities?

___

2. How can you "diversify" your approach to excellence by seeking growth and improvement in various aspects of your life, personally and professionally?

___

3. What are the long-term "returns" of investing in a life of excellence and consistently striving to be your best for God's glory?

___

Word Wealth Builder

"I can do all things through Christ who strengthens me." (Philippians 4:13 NKJV)

This empowering verse reminds us that our ability to excel and achieve great things is not based on our strength or talent but on the power of Christ working in and through us. As we rely on Him and draw from His inexhaustible resources, we find the courage and capacity to pursue excellence in every area of our lives.

Growth Fund

1. How has your understanding and pursuit of excellence grown over the past year? What challenges or victories have shaped your perspective?

___

2. In what areas do you desire further growth in your ability to excel and maximize your God-given potential? What steps can you take to facilitate that growth?

___

3. How can you use your learning journey to pursue excellence to encourage and inspire others in their walk with God?

___

Optimization Strategy

Develop an "Excellence Action Plan." Identify one area of your life where you believe God is calling you to grow and excel (e.g., a skill, a character trait, a ministry role). Create a practical plan for pursuing excellence in that area, including setting specific goals, identifying necessary resources or training, and establishing accountability with a mentor or coach. Commit to implementing this plan over the next 90 days, tracking your progress, and celebrating your growth.

Prayer Maximizer

Father, I come before You today, recognizing that You have created me with unique talents, abilities, and potential. I thank You for the opportunity to pursue excellence and make the most of the gifts You have entrusted to me. Forgive me for the times I have settled for mediocrity or allowed fear and self-doubt to hold me back from fully embracing Your plans and purposes for my life. Renew my mind and heart, replacing any limiting beliefs with the truth of Your Word and the empowering presence of Your Spirit. Give me the courage to step out in faith, pursuing excellence in every area of my life as an act of worship and service to You. Help me to view challenges and obstacles as opportunities for growth and refinement, trusting in Your strength and wisdom to guide me forward. May my pursuit of excellence bring glory to Your name and inspire others to discover and develop the potential You have placed within them. In Jesus' name, Amen.

Chapter 10: The Responsibility of Stewardship

Stewardship is a fundamental concept in our spiritual journey, recognizing that all we have our time, talents, resources, and even our very lives ultimately belong to God. We are not owners, but managers entrusted with the responsibility of using what God has given us to further His kingdom and bring glory to His name. Coupled with stewardship is the powerful attitude of gratitude, which enables us to be better stewards of God's gifts and positions us to receive even more of His blessings and favor.

Credit Repair

1. In what areas do you struggle with a lack of stewardship or tendency to view your resources as your own?

_____
_____
_____

2. How have past mistakes or mismanagement affected your view of stewardship and your ability to trust God with your resources?

_____
_____
_____

3. What truths from God's Word can you use to "repair" any faulty beliefs or attitudes about stewardship and your role as a manager of God's blessings?

_____
_____
_____

Savings Deposit

1. Reflect on when you experienced the joy and blessing of faithfully stewarding a resource or opportunity God entrusted you. What lessons did you learn from that experience?

_____
_____
_____

2. What are some biblical promises and truths about the rewards of good stewardship that you can "deposit" into your heart and mind?

_____
_____

3. How can you "invest" in your stewardship by seeking wisdom and guidance from God in managing your time, talents, and resources?

___

___

___

Investment Portfolio

1. What are some specific areas of your life where you need to "invest" more intentional stewardship and wise management of your resources?

___

___

___

___

2. How can you "diversify" your approach to stewardship by exploring creative ways to use your time, talents, and resources for God's kingdom purposes?

___

___

___

___

3. What are the long-term "returns" of investing in a lifestyle of faithful stewardship and consistently seeking to honor God with all He has entrusted to you?

___

___

___

___

Word Wealth Builder

"Moreover it is required in stewards that one be found faithful." (1 Corinthians 4:2 NKJV)

This concise yet powerful verse encapsulates the essence of stewardship. As managers of God's resources, our primary goal is not to achieve worldly success or accumulate personal wealth but rather to be found faithful in fulfilling the responsibilities He has entrusted to us. As we prioritize faithfulness in our stewardship, we can trust that God will honor and bless our efforts for His glory.

Growth Fund

1. How has your understanding and practice of stewardship grown over the past year? What challenges or victories have shaped your perspective?

   _____
   _____
   _____
   _____

2. What areas do you desire further growth in maintaining a grateful heart, regardless of your circumstances? What steps can you take to facilitate that growth?

   _____
   _____
   _____
   _____

3. How can you use your learning journey to embrace stewardship to encourage and inspire others in their walk with God?

   _____
   _____
   _____
   _____

Optimization Strategy

Conduct a "Stewardship Audit." Take some time to prayerfully reflect on the various resources God has entrusted to you (e.g., time, talents, finances, relationships). Write each one down, and then, next to each, evaluate your current level of stewardship and identify areas where you can improve. Develop a practical plan for enhancing stewardship in each area, setting specific goals and action steps. Commit to implementing this plan over the next quarter, regularly assessing your progress and making necessary adjustments.

Prayer Maximizer

Father, I come before You today, acknowledging that every good and perfect gift comes from You. I thank You for the incredible privilege and responsibility of stewarding Your resources. Forgive me for the times I have viewed these blessings as my own or failed to use them in ways that honor and glorify You. Renew my mind and heart, aligning them with Your purposes and plans for the resources entrusted to me. Give me the wisdom, courage, and faithfulness to be a good steward in every area of my life – my time, talents, finances, and relationships. Help me to hold loosely to the things of this world, always ready to use them for Your kingdom purposes and the advancement of Your will. Renew my mind and heart, replacing any seeds of discontentment or entitlement with a deep-rooted gratitude that permeates every area of my life. May my stewardship be a testimony to Your goodness and generosity, inspiring others to trust You more deeply with all that they have. In Jesus' name, Amen.

Conclusion

As you come to the end of this workbook, I hope that you have discovered the incredible power and potential of raising your heavenly FICO SCORES. Throughout these pages, you have explored 10 key principles that have the ability to transform your life and deepen your relationship with God.

But this is not the end of your journey; it is just the beginning. The principles and truths you have encountered in this workbook are not meant to be simply absorbed and filed away, but rather to be lived out and applied in your daily life.

As you continue on your path of spiritual growth, remember to keep investing in your relationship with God. Make time for prayer, study His Word, and seek His will in all things. Surround yourself with a community of believers who will encourage, challenge, and support you in your walk with Christ.

When challenges and obstacles arise, hold fast to the truths you have learned and the promises of God. Remember that He is faithful, and that He is working all things together for your good and His glory.

Above all, keep your eyes fixed on Jesus, the Author and Perfecter of your faith. He is the one who began this good work in you, and He will carry it on to completion until the day of His return.

As you continue to raise your heavenly FICO SCORES, may you experience the fullness of God's love, grace, and power in your life. May you be a light in this world, reflecting the goodness and glory of God to all those around you.

Thank you for joining me on this journey of transformation and growth. May God bless you abundantly as you seek to honor Him with every aspect of your life, and may your heavenly FICO SCORES continue to rise as you walk in obedience and faith.

> *The grace of the Lord Jesus Christ, and the love of God, and the [a]communion of the Holy Spirit be with you all. Amen. (2 Corinthians 13:14)*

www.ingramcontent.com/pod-product-compliance
Lightning Source LLC
LaVergne TN
LVHW061325060426
835507LV00019B/2302